MORE THAN

MORE THAN

>

MIGHTY MEN OF GOD
Independent Publishing with Createspace at Amazon.com

MORE THAN

Instigator: Ken Wenner
Cover design by: Luke Neil

Independent publishing with Createspace at amazon.com

©Be More With Jesus
www.bemorewithjesus.com

**All scripture quotations used in this book are from
The Holy Bible New International Version
Unless noted**

PRINTED IN THE UNITED STATES OF AMERICA

T

ISBN-13: **978-0615584607** (Custom Universal) ISBN-10: **0615584608**

There was a group of 8 men who participated in this production. They are listed in the back

MORE THAN

Message from the instigator

Write a book?!
That was my comment while praying to God about reaching out to more men.

You see our senior pastor is always impressing upon us to reach out to more men at our monthly men's breakfast and our yearly men's conference. He would say...I want to see 100 men at breakfast! At conference time the comments would be, I want to get 200 men to our conference. What can we do to reach out to the men of this church?

So I'm praying one night while I rock my 1 ½ year old son to sleep, Lord... how do we reach these men? As a matter of fact why stop there? How about 1000 men, how about 10,000, how about 1,000,000 men?

And then cometh the answer...Write a book. Oh I argued! I hardly read books (except the bible and not often enough), I don't have time for that!! What should we right about? A men's devotional I hear. We don't need any more of those! You can't retain a thing, you fall behind on your readings, etc, etc...God's response. Take it to the Monday night men's group, make it a weekly read, a verse a week with the writers' thoughts included with the verse.

The good Lord had spoken!

A year and a half later we have a moving, inspirational, emotional, motivational, weekly read, for men brought to you by men who battle every day the lies of the enemy. Some of us didn't believe we had anything good to offer...we didn't have anything that could help another man. Well the devils a liar!

Eight of us give you a small portion of some of our favorite verses and the light those verses have shed on our lives for you to read, think about, pray through, then hopefully grow in your faith and belief and change your heart!

We are more than our insecurities, more than the battles we face, more than our failures, more than the lies of the enemy, **MORE THAN CONQUERORS!**

Contents

Contents

Salvation

John 3:16

For God so loved the world that he gave his one and only Son, that whoever believes in him shall not perish but have eternal life.

God loved us so much, he gave all to display his love for us. You see, he gave His one and only son. The most amazing fact is that He gave it all and still gives us the choice to decide on whether to accept Him or not. He simply gave it all so that you and I would have the chance of eternal life. We need to understand that we are God's masterpiece. There is no greater love beyond this.

This single verse is simply the key to heaven, to our acceptance of Jesus as our personal savior and to have eternal life with God the father. As a very young boy, with much uncertainty, I learned this truth and it has been the force that has carried me through my life's journey. As a father of my own children now, this truth is even more meaningful and powerful than ever.

This verse prompts us to answer these questions:
Do I believe in God? Do I believe in Jesus? Do I know how much God loves me?
If you have not, would you consider accepting him today? Would you consider that He shed his blood for you? Would you consider that he loves you much more than anyone will ever do? He desires to have relationship with you. Yes, with you! All you have to do is accept His love.

RG

What are the lessons God has for me in this passage of scripture?

_____

_____

_____

_____

Can I truly feel Gods love for me?

_____

_____

_____

_____

NOTES

_____

_____

_____

_____

_____

_____

Prayer

_____

_____

_____

_____

5 Minutes Minimum

Ephesians 5:25

"Husbands, love your wives, just as Christ loved the church and gave himself up for her...."

For many men it is hard to pray for their wives. I confess it was hard for me too, but it is so important to the health and strength of my marriage. Do you pray for your wife daily? Maybe a couple of sentences, or even 30 seconds? But what if you prayed for your wife for **5 minutes minimum** each day? Those 5 minutes can change your marriage and change your life. Why do you pray? You are her covering. The Lord has put you together and she is yours to take care of...regardless of how you might feel at times. If your marriage is having challenges this 5 minutes might be all the more important. It may not be easy at first, even feeling uncomfortable but it is worth it.

Make a list of prayer topics, Think about her day. What is she going through, what are her strengths and challenges? When making the list, try to look at her through Jesus' eyes and not your own. Sometimes our hurts and scars can distort our perspective. Dedicate to her 5 short minutes lifting her up to the Lord. Be purposeful, be diligent, have faith and believe in the One you are praying to. Pray with truthfulness, be honest with the Lord.

Listen; my wife and I have had our struggles. I'm sure a lot of the same struggles most people have in a marriage. Me devoting this minimum prayer time has been a blessing for me and my attitude alone. When I do know what her day is going to be like and I lay it down before the Lord I can see a difference at the end of the day
Your attitude **will** change towards her. Focusing this much attention to areas in her life that need prayer support will change your attitude. Irritations will be softened. Miracles will begin happening in her life. You will begin to see answers to your prayers. You want to save/rebuild your marriage? Pray to the One who has the power to supernaturally change and heal hearts. Miracle transformation comes from the Lord.

Want change? Take it to the Lord. She may just be praying for you too.
LN

2

What are the lessons God has for me in this passage of scripture?

_____

_____

_____

_____

How could my life be blessed praying for my wife?

_____

_____

_____

_____

NOTES

_____

_____

_____

_____

_____

_____

_____

Prayer

_____

_____

_____

Give Up Your Worries

Philippians 4:6-7

Do not be anxious about anything, but in every situation, by prayer and petition, with thanksgiving, present your requests to God. And the peace of God, which transcends all understanding, will guard your hearts and your minds in Christ Jesus.

God speaks directly into our hearts via the apostle Paul and calls us to not worry about the physical, emotional, social and financial challenges that we may confront daily.

We must present, lay down and handover sincerely, our needs to God and depend totally on Him in order to overcome. But most importantly, we must give God thanks in the process regardless of our situation at the present time.

Unhappiness, emotional distress and all dysfunctional behavior arises from an individual's inability to find a consistent way to meet his/her human needs, in a positive way. It is now that we must understand that Christ is the author of who we are, that he knows what it feels like and that he wants us to give him not only our needs but all the glory. If we would only choose to taste the peace of God, which transcends all understanding, and trust Him. He promises not only to resolve our challenges, but to guard our hearts way beyond our understanding or expectation.

Why oh why is this difficult? Present your request to God! Oh when I really walk in this!! It is a wonderful feeling. Don't think that as a writer in this book I have it all figured out. I struggle day in and day out with the same issues as any man.

So my friend, would you trust God today? Would you hand him your needs today?
RG

What are the lessons God has for me in this passage of scripture?

_____

_____

_____

_____

How can I avoid stress & unhappiness daily, all day?

_____

_____

_____

_____

NOTES

_____

_____

_____

_____

_____

_____

_____

Prayer

_____

_____

_____

_____

His Kingdom our Home

Psalm 27:1

> **The LORD is my light and my salvation— whom shall I fear?**
> **The LORD is the stronghold of my life— of whom shall I be afraid?**

David had experiences that were incredibly difficult. He was thrown out of his own kingdom, was slandered and betrayed by the son he loved, that very son was killed by one of his associates, and of course he also faced the conviction of his own sins. And yet his heart sang forth: "The Lord is my light and my salvation – whom shall I fear?". For years there was a battle raging inside myself, I mean really raging. Like David, there was so much 'turmoil' outside of my control. But, for me it was actually inside my mind and my heart. I didn't even know what the battle was about until in my young adult life it became clear that I had an unhealthy struggle with needing acceptance, to the point that the fear of rejection consumed me. Even in a full stupor there seemed to be that one message that beamed through the fog of alcohol "you do not fit in, you are not accepted".

But when I accepted Christ into my heart I instantly realized that I was a part of something, something eternal, something bigger than anything on earth. The Lord became my salvation, my stronghold, my refuge, my assurance, my confidence. It felt as if I had gone from quick sand to standing on a rock. Clarity broke through, I actually am an 'alien' on earth, just passing through; But I am fully accepted by the king of the universe.

Over the years the old record plays again and I hear "You belong to no one. You are not loved." The volume may be low but I hear it and it affects how I act – and more so how I feel inside as I interact with people. When that happens I fight by repeating Psalm 27:1 and by knowing I am a child of God, he is the purpose of my life, he is who I live for. With him on my side, what can a man do to me? God desires for Jesus to be your refuge, your strength, the joy in your life, to be the rock on which you stand. To overcome your struggles and the old patterns of thinking that make you feel trapped, helpless, or call you to serve them. Would you courageously reveal your heart to Jesus? Will you reveal to him the place that hurts, the place you know needs to be changed, and take it to Him in prayer? He will be your rock!

MB

What are the lessons God has for me in this passage of scripture?

_____

_____

_____

_____

What will it take for me to feel that spiritual breakthrough?

_____

_____

_____

_____

NOTES

_____

_____

_____

_____

_____

_____

Prayer

_____

_____

_____

Go Ahead, Challenge Me

Judges 6:37-40

Look, I will place a wool fleece on the threshing floor. If there is dew only on the fleece and all the ground is dry, then I will know that you will save Israel by my hand, as you said. And that is what happened. Gideon rose early the next day; he squeezed the fleece and wrung out the dew-a bowlful of water. Then Gideon said to God, "Do not be angry with me. Let me make just one more request. Allow me one more test with the fleece. This time make the fleece dry and the ground covered with dew." That night God did so. Only the fleece was dry; all the ground was covered.

These verses make me laugh when I first read them, Gideon just wants to make sure what God said to him is true. But then it is not enough, this type of challenge of God's word goes on and on throughout the Bible! Here God says what he will do for Gideon and Israel, Gideon says OK, but...just to make sure I understand... and then of course, God meets the request. But... Gideon wants to double, make that triple check the word of God. Of course, God is grace, and mercy!

These lessons are in the Bible for us today, so we can see that some of the most historical figures in biblical times still couldn't believe sometimes, still felt inadequate to do the work of God perhaps. Personally, I still challenge God regularly, He has proved himself over and over, starting with my own life, my wife, my kids, the life I live (and it is a challenge), all given to me by God! Yet I question the path he has me on? Every day I try to hear what God wants me to hear wherever I am. Driving and listening to the radio, listening at a business meeting, listening to a friend, listening to our pastor. Then, I try to believe and not challenge, or try to put more to it.

Hear this week what God is saying to you and believe Him. Don't challenge Him! What can you do by God's hand?

KW

5

What are the lessons God has for me in this passage of scripture?

_____

_____

_____

_____

How often am I asking God to prove himself?

_____

_____

_____

_____

NOTES

_____

_____

_____

_____

_____

_____

_____

Prayer

_____

_____

_____

_____

Stand Firm

1 Corinthians 15:58

"Therefore my dear brothers, stand firm. Let nothing move you. Always give yourselves fully to the work of the Lord, because you know that your labor in the Lord is not in vain"

Our lord is encouraging us, brothers, to stand firm for our adventure with God, placing ourselves on the rock of Christ so nothing can move us. To surrender it all to Him so His light will always shine on us and through us. To choose the TRUTH through our Father God so we can rest in His labor.

In order to achieve this personally, I have PURPOSED to live this out every day, starting with making my morning devotional and prayer time a MUST before I start my day. Allowing God access to my heart every day to guide, shape, and direct me in this journey.

My goal as a man of God is to become all that God created me to be, and, to live His adventure with purpose. So in order to do this, I must stay connected to Him every day! This isn't something I learned overnight, and the changes didn't come overnight. I had to PURPOSE TO LIVE THIS OUT EVERY DAY! I had to keep focused on God knowing his will in my life was for good.

So today, I challenge you to clear your schedule each morning and spend that valuable time with your Father God. Even if this means you have to get up earlier or change your schedule.

This adventure is yours to be had! Purpose to be a man of God, the leader in your household!

MH

What are the lessons God has for me in this passage of scripture?

_____

_____

_____

_____

Things I can change to make that time.

_____

_____

_____

_____

NOTES

_____

_____

_____

_____

_____

_____

_____

Prayer

_____

_____

_____

_____

Remember the Simple Miracles

2nd Corinthians 4:8,9,10

We are hard pressed on every side, but not crushed: Perplexed, but not in despair; Persecuted, but not abandoned; Struck down, but not destroyed. We always carry around in our body the death of Jesus. So that the life of Jesus may also be revealed in our body!

In our daily life we can be hard pressed, we can be perplexed, we can be abandoned, struck down. But with the Holy Spirit ever present in our hearts we are not crushed, nor in despair, nor abandoned, nor destroyed.

Just emailed this to a friend who posted on his Facebook page that "things just went from bad to worse way way too fast"! The word of God is powerful! We need to read it and believe it! That's it! When I heard our Pastor preach this verse for the first time it was like a revelation! I had no idea that, to not understand was OK. And believe me there is a lot I don't understand, but I don't let it drive me to despair!!

Just read it and live it! Don't complain about the tough things this week. You don't have to understand why they are the way they are! Give God praise for waking up, breathing air, seeing in color, walking on your own two feet, thinking with your right mind, having ten fingers and toes!! These we take advantage of! Start with that and see how the week goes! When someone asks how you're doing, tell em'... GREAT!! Woke up breathing air this morning!!

KW

What are the lessons God has for me in this passage of scripture?

_____

_____

_____

_____

What steps can I take to remember this verse during the week?

_____

_____

_____

_____

NOTES

_____

_____

_____

_____

_____

_____

Prayer

_____

_____

_____

Whose Plan is it?

Jeremiah 29:11-13

For I know the plans I have for you, "declares the Lord," plans to prosper you and not to harm you, plans to give you hope and a future. Then you will call upon me and come and pray to me, and I will listen to you. You will seek me and find me when you seek me with all your heart.

God knows the plans he has for us! "declares the Lord"! Not, WE know the plan, HE knows the plan!!

My personal plan hit the dirt quite soon after my wife and I married. We bought a house, started to plan for a family (in the future), first, just be together, watch football on the weekends, take some nice vacations. Then... barely a year into our marriage we got a nine year old, a boy, six months later another almost nine year old, a girl. My wife's sister's kids. This was thirteen years ago my plan hit the dirt. The kids are 20 something now, it hasn't been bad. Difficult? Sure! Mostly it just was not my plan.

Not the most popular but the most powerful part of this very popular chapter and verse of the Bible. *"You will seek me and FIND me when you seek me with all your heart."* ALL your heart! Through this last thirteen years (as I stated it hasn't been bad) I have found myself regularly really praying for some understanding with all my heart. I have then found myself more than willing to operate within Gods plan.

Try it, see what he will do if you leave it in his hands! Seek God this week with all your heart! He will listen to you. His plans are to give you hope and a future.

KW

What are the lessons God has for me in this passage of scripture?

_____

_____

_____

_____

How do I follow Gods plan? How do I know his plan?

_____

_____

_____

_____

NOTES

_____

_____

_____

_____

_____

_____

_____

Prayer

_____

_____

_____

_____

No Expectations

John 2:23-25

Now while he was in Jerusalem at the Passover Festival, many people saw the signs he was performing and believed in his name. But Jesus would not entrust himself to them, for he knew all people. He did not need any testimony about mankind, for he knew what was in each person.

Here we see that Jesus (the true example of love) loved without expecting back as He "knew what was in each person." True obedience is truly freeing and there is only one person we should trust in and be obedient to, Jesus. Doing so we can then follow Him and His ways. Giving to others what he calls us to give.

For years I sought approval of men/women, it was easy to give love because I would usually receive love back. When I didn't get love back, to justify the rejection, I would build up arguments and disgust for people to avoid the disappointment and pain.

Regardless and in spite of what people give to us (good or bad) we are to love each other with the love He shows us, we are to comfort others with the comfort we ourselves have been given, and we are to forgive others as God (through Jesus) has completely forgiven us. We are to be obedient in all these things by dying to ourselves, and by being powered by His love of us and our love for Him.

MB

What are the lessons God has for me in this passage of scripture?

_____

_____

_____

_____

What can I do to practice forgiveness?

_____

_____

_____

_____

NOTES

_____

_____

_____

_____

_____

_____

Prayer

_____

_____

_____

"I" Can Do Nothing

John 15:5

"I am the vine; you are the branches. If you remain in me and I in you, you will bear much fruit; apart from me you can do nothing.

The part that rings loudest in my ear is "apart from me you can do nothing." And what is it to bear fruit? Show the joy, the love of God. Reach out to others. Be an answer to prayer...

In my short time knowing Jesus I know that the fruit that I bear because of him tastes better, looks better, and the smallest bite can feed the hungriest of men. I would rather bear one small piece of fruit that has God's blessing than an entire vineyard of fruit without it. Laying down my life and letting him truly be the author has made me realize that I can not do anything without him. If I try, I always mess it up. A morning blessed by Jesus makes the whole day better. . .
A day without his blessing is a stern reminder of the past and my past is a clear demonstration of struggling with evil. We are not alone in this world, no matter what, because we have him and he loves us more than any of us could love anything. We can't even begin to understand his love for us. Apart from him we can do nothing but if we remain in him, he will remain in us and that means that with him we can do anything!!!

Praise Jesus. I am so thankful for the trials and tribulations that you gifted me Lord, without them I would not have found you and without you I am nothing.

RS

What are the lessons God has for me in this passage of scripture?

_____

_____

_____

_____

What can I do to practice forgiveness?

_____

_____

_____

_____

NOTES

_____

_____

_____

_____

_____

_____

_____

Prayer

_____

_____

_____

_____

Run The Race

Acts 5:35-39

"Men of Israel, consider carefully what you intend to do to these men. Some time ago Theudas appeared, claiming to be somebody, and about four hundred men rallied to him. He was killed, all his followers were dispersed, and it all came to nothing._After him, Judas the Galilean appeared in the days of the census and led a band of people in revolt. He too was killed, and all his followers were scattered. Therefore, in the present case I advise you: Leave these men alone! Let them go! For if their purpose or activity is of human origin, it will fail. But if it is from God, you will not be able to stop these men; you will only find yourselves fighting against God."

If our purpose and activity is of human origin; we will fail. If our purpose or activity is from God; nothing can stop it. **Any hurdle in the race of life that presents itself is an opportunity to learn,** an opportunity that God has created for us to trust in him. If we trip on a hurdle we may not win the race but if we allow God to pick us up we will finish. When we stop at the hurdles of life and try to figure out why they are there, how to get around them, or how to go under them, we are not trusting that God has already thought of a way for us to get over them. We essentially are fighting against God, a battle which cannot be won.

Right now I feel like nothing can stop me! Well, most of the time, OK sometimes, OK I know this: my purpose is of God and He will not let me fail! And if you go against me you WILL find yourself fighting against God!
Make your day purposeful, know that you can do what God has planned!
"without him I can do nothing but with him the possibilities are endless".
RS

What are the lessons God has for me in this passage of scripture?

_____

_____

_____

_____

Am I fighting against something now?

_____

_____

_____

_____

NOTES

_____

_____

_____

_____

_____

_____

Prayer

_____

_____

_____

_____

Pick i✝ up

Matthew 16:24

Then Jesus said "Whoever wants to be my disciple must deny themselves and take up their cross and follow me"

Jesus always has a way with words. In Matthew 16 starting with the 24th verse, we see how Jesus wants us to follow him, what he wants us to consider and do.

We have to **let Jesus lead! We are no longer the leaders of our lives. We have to let Him be in charge and in control. We are no longer in the driver's seat, He is.**
Let us think of a game of chess where it is us against the devil. We need to not only trust God to play the moves for us, but we also have to give him all our pieces.

I reflect back on the homeowners association of our neighborhood calling for me to participate as president and the tugging I kept feeling from God calling me to step into the roll as well. I kept saying, God I am not ready yet, I haven't been trained for it yet. But that didn't stop him. I recall the struggle of doing what God was calling me to, versus what the enemy was lying to me about. Until one day, alone at the gym, at the pool and hearing God giving me the options I can be the president or I can be nothing, I get to choose. At that moment I realized that something bigger than me was at hand. At that moment I had a divine encounter and made the decision that I would do it God's way! And that even though I didn't think I had everything that was needed or wasn't good enough, I knew He was and that all things are possible for those who believe. I had to take my hands of the wheel and allow God to take control of my life. Looking back, He had a plan and purpose for the huge transitions that were about to take place and that He had put me there for such a day and such a time. I lead the association through major changes in staffing and process, things that only by God's grace and blessings was I able to do. So don't hesitate when God calls you. Trust Him and watch what He can do through your hands, your gifts, your talents, and your willingness to serve.
God knows the beginning from the end and knows what move to make and what the upcoming moves need to be. We need to trust Him with all of our life, all of the pieces. We need to hand them over to our Lord and Savior who we are to follow.

PD

What are the lessons God has for me in this passage of scripture?

_____

_____

_____

_____

How can I deny myself?

_____

_____

_____

_____

NOTES

_____

_____

_____

_____

_____

_____

_____

Prayer

_____

_____

_____

_____

Embrace the Challenge

Matthew 16:25

Jesus still says "For whoever wants to save their life will lose it, but whoever loses their life for me will find it."

We aren't supposed to run from suffering, but to embrace it. If we follow Jesus, He will show us how.
We go through hard times to help develop the character that Jesus wants us to develop. I heard a sermon on the beach a few months back and I felt that the pastor was talking right to me as I was trying to decide if I should leave the comfortable job I had grown into, had built relationships in, had made it through trials in, that had gotten me to this point of my life. During the sermon, he said "God didn't make it so we would be comfortable: He wants to build character." Wow, that hit home and when I look back at the last few teams I have worked with on the job I could see that the hard times, were preparation for the time that was to come. So needless to say, I am in the new job. God had opened the door, and not even I could close it, but decided to walk through it. Amen.

Get uncomfortable, reach farther, do more, God does have more for you than you can hope for or imagine! Believe it, apply it!

PD

What are the lessons God has for me in this passage of scripture?

_____

_____

_____

_____

What is my comfort level? Am I missing anything?

_____

_____

_____

_____

NOTES

_____

_____

_____

_____

_____

_____

_____

Prayer

_____

_____

_____

_____

Believe

John 14: 8, 9

**Phillip said, "Lord show us the Father and that will be enough for us."
Jesus answered, "Don't you know me, Phillip, even after I have been among you such a long time? Anyone who has seen me has seen the Father. How can you say, 'Show us the Father?'**

To really grasp the magnitude of such a request you have to look at John 21:25, which states, *"Jesus did many other miracles as well. If everyone of them were written down, I suppose that even the **whole** world would not have enough room for the books that would be written."*
Now Philip who has seen not only the miracles performed by Jesus that have been documented, but also... all those that there wouldn't be room for in the "whole world." And he wants to see the father for more proof that Jesus is the son of God! NO HE DOES NOT? Is that disrespectful? You know what? I'm the same way! I don't appreciate anything that God has given me! I find myself disappointed, discouraged, disgusted, annoyed, bitter...even frustrated with the things I have been given. Effortless feelings I call them.
Make the choice this week that the miracles you have in your life are just that, miracles!! Live in the Holy Spirit full of peace, joy, happiness. Throw down those effortless feelings. Make the effort!

KW

What are the lessons God has for me in this passage of scripture?

_____

_____

_____

_____

List the miracles in your life.

_____

_____

_____

_____

NOTES

_____

_____

_____

_____

_____

_____

_____

Prayer

_____

_____

_____

_____

What are you Hearing Today?

Isaiah 59:17 NLT

"He puts on righteousness as his body armor and places the helmet of salvation on his head. He clothed himself with a robe of vengeance and wrapped himself in a cloak of divine passion"

Wow, just think if every man did that every morning. How our days would be? Start with the righteousness of body armor instead of a cup or pot of coffee...then place the helmet of salvation on your head, not an egg muffin or bagel with cream cheese in your mouth! Clothe yourselves with a robe of vengeance instead of driving off to work with 45 minutes of road rage and the day full of responsibility. Wrap yourself in a cloak of divine passion...oooh that's good! It's wrapped, not put on, thrown on, or hung on the body, it's WRAPPED, to protect and cover the WHOLE body.
 Now that is some passion. Just think if you could walk every day with passion in your life. Everything you do would be WITH passion. I know that would help me through my day. Don't you? But, unfortunately, most of us don't do that.

"Modern man 59:17" definition: He puts on the TO DO's of the day as his body armor and places the helmet of DUTY on his head. He clothes himself with a robe of RESPONSIBILITY and wraps himself in a cloak of complete EXHAUSTION. Does that ring a bit true for you today? Sadly, it is all too true for most men living today.
 Every morning I wake up, get the coffee going and stop...and pray, first for my wife for at least 5 minutes, then the family, then for the rest of the day that comes roaring after me. Before I started doing so, the day seemed hard at most every turn and especially exhausting. More than ever I see the things that God sees, not continually but it is a growing part of my day. I have a vision for what he wants me to do and road blocks seem minor as I just keep moving forward. My heart is changing.

As men, we need to find our divine passion in life. To wake up, and have our masculinity back. Open the door and have that adventure outside the concrete jungle that God created us to have. Ask and seek God in this question for your life..."what is my holy passion?" God tells us when we seek, we shall find.
We as men, in order to be fulfilled, GOD fulfilled, need to just find the "right clothes" to put on, amen? AMEN!

MH

What are the lessons God has for me in this passage of scripture?

_____

_____

_____

_____

What is my 1st step to making the change?

_____

_____

_____

_____

NOTES

_____

_____

_____

_____

_____

_____

_____

Prayer

_____

_____

_____

_____

Freedom By Faith

2 Corinthians 5:7 ‑ "For we live by faith, not by sight."

What do I see? I see that the job I have could end abruptly and throw my financial life into disarray. This is a tough job market and it would be difficult to find a job like the one I have. When I am focused on keeping or preserving my job, a job at times that requires way more than I know or can give, my creativity is hampered and my relationships with co-workers changes to one of 'safety' rather than purpose. When I focus on what I see, I walk in worry.

Psalms 55:22

Cast your cares on the Lord and he will sustain you; He will never let the righteous fall.

But faith tells me something very different........that God is big enough to take all of my cares and He will do so if I cast my burdens on him for He is strong enough to carry them all. Faith knows God is my provider and is the same yesterday, today and tomorrow. Did He not give me this job? Has He not provided for me all these years? Why doubt Him now? When I give him my cares, I am light hearted, care more about others, listen better, am more creative, and understand clearly how much God has put me where I am for a particular purpose. I can walk in confidence that He will sustain me and hold me up.

I don't think there is a man alive that doesn't carry some burden(s). Yet our Lord doesn't say to cast 'some' cares, he says to cast our cares on him, whatever we have. Will you do that today, and every day, literally take your worries, problems, concerns, and burdens in your hands and 'cast' them at His feet while claiming His promise in Psalm 55:22? If the worries come up a second time, again cast them at His feet, and keep doing it each time they come up. There is such freedom He offers each one of us. He wants so much for you to be free! Thank you Jesus for your promises and your faithfulness – How I need you to walk in freedom!

MB

What are the lessons God has for me in this passage of scripture?

_____

_____

_____

_____

List your worries.

_____

_____

_____

_____

NOTES

_____

_____

_____

_____

_____

_____

_____

Prayer

_____

_____

_____

_____

Walk By Faith

2 Corinthians 5:7 - **"For we live by faith, not by sight."**

What do I see? I see that the more I get to know people, the more I see how messed up they are. They have problems and most of the time it affects me... but even if it doesn't, it would seem they really do some stupid things; have stupid attitudes; and think stupid ways. I know I am not perfect and I make mistakes. But really, those other people are really messed up!

James 3:9–11
With the tongue we praise our Lord and Father, and with it we curse men, who have been made in God's likeness. Out of the same mouth comes praise and cursing. My brothers, this should not be. Can both fresh water and salt water flow from the same spring?

Romans 2:11
For God does not show favoritism.

But faith tells me something very different........ God loves each and every one of us just the same. He does not show favoritism regardless of the 'stupid' things we do. We were all made in his image. He doesn't bring rain, the sun, and his son to just some of his children but to all of them. How can praise to him be clean and honorable when from the same mouth we slander his very creation. Those that, by the way, are our brothers and sisters in creation?
We must seek to love others as we love ourselves. Do we not 'cut ourselves slack'? Have I not done the very same thing that I complain others do? My brothers and sisters in Christ are on a journey just like me! Remember where I started? Yikes!!!! I am so glad Christ chose me and I still need Him so much! I am so glad that he doesn't give up on me and keeps working on me. And now he calls me to not give up on others either! Rather he calls me to spur them toward love and good deeds

Will you join me in sharing the love that God has for everyone! Will you fear the Lord and put to death your flesh that wants so much to belittle or say bad things about others?
Lord, forgive me for my arrogance, for thinking I know what I think I know. I am so happy that your ways are so much better than mine. Lord, keep my ears open and my heart full of love for others.

MB

What are the lessons God has for me in this passage of scripture?

_____

_____

_____

_____

What can I do 1st to release my judgmental mindset?

_____

_____

_____

_____

NOTES

_____

_____

_____

_____

_____

_____

Prayer

_____

_____

_____

_____

Wealth By Faith

2 Corinthians 5:7 - **"For we live by faith, not by sight."**

What do I see? I try really hard to do the right things and by the power of Jesus. As much as I can remember to do so. But when I look at how many people around me, non-believers (some of which really don't even try to do the right thing, and certainly not for Jesus) seem to have it made, I get really frustrated. It just doesn't seem ... well... fair. Why do they have an easy time speaking, get paid the big bucks, drive the nice cars, live in the nice homes, and have families that seem to have it all together? Why does everything seem so easy for them? I know it is wrong to envy but sometimes it is so blatant the thoughts seem unavoidable.

James 2:5

"Listen, my dear brothers and sisters: Has not God chosen those who are poor in the eyes of the world to be rich in faith and to inherit the kingdom he promised those who love him?"

But faith tells me something very different....... Okay, now wait a minute. Which crown do I want? One of gold and jewels that will fade away like a wild flower. Or a crown of life that the Lord will give me. Do I want to please my flesh or please my God?

Is our heavenly father so unlike an earthly father who wants to give us good things? As a father myself, what do I want most for my children? First and foremost, I want a deep relationship with them. I want to know them and I want them to know me. I want to see that my children have character and a belief that I will do good things for them, that I love them (not having suspicion of me that I am trying to catch them doing something wrong so I can punish them). And the fruit of such things is a fearless attitude, a bold and adventurous spirit, yet one of respect for those around them. I want to see kindness and gentleness, learning and understanding, and a loving nature radiating from them. Do I want them to be wealthy? I do, but only if it does not corrupt their character.
If this is the heart of me, a father made of flesh, how much more true and right and beneficial must be Gods desire for us?

Do you envy someone's position, wealth, boat, job, or maybe even their wife? Call out right now to your heavenly father.............. LORD I NEED YOU! Forgive me for my envy. You have me right where I need to be. I trust you. I accept your will for my life and I will seek to do your will where I am at and not be distracted by my fleshly desires Lord I need you and I trust you. I refuse to let things govern over me – for YOU are my Lord!

MB

18

What are the lessons God has for me in this passage of scripture?

_____

_____

_____

_____

What do I do with my money?

_____

_____

_____

_____

NOTES

_____

_____

_____

_____

_____

_____

Prayer

_____

_____

_____

_____

Sight By Faith

Corinthians 5:7 - "For we live by faith, not by sight."

What do I see? When I grew up it was the tall teenagers that always got the attention and compliments from those around me. I would hear things from adults like "Wow, look how tall that young man is" or "Isn't he growing up quick and handsome." And it was the beautiful girls that my friends and I wanted to hang around with. And today in the business world the same things take place. And how many of us men struggle with lust? We all do! Some might argue whether it is a sin or not because it is so "natural." But I know that anything I do, any thought I have that draws me away from God's holiness is a sin. He created us to be like him in true righteousness and holiness.

1 Samuel 16:7

But the LORD said to Samuel, "Do not consider his appearance or his height, for I have rejected him. The LORD does not look at the things people look at. People look at the outward appearance, but the LORD looks at the heart."

But faith tells me something very different..... I look at the outside but God reminds me that what is important and what I should be looking at is the person's heart. If I am looking at the outside of the person and what I want from the person (to look at their beauty or to lust after them), how can I see or pay attention to what the person needs? How can I serve that person? So by faith, by 'crucifying' the thought of lust, by nailing it to the cross as it comes into my mind (knowing that Christ already paid the ultimate price for each of my sinful thoughts), and by casting down my imaginations that exalt themselves above God the Holy Spirit puts in me a holy love for the person. I then can serve them (truly love them) without any distracting thoughts.
Do you want to live where you are at today? Or do you have a desire to be totally free to serve the Lord so you can hear those precious words from Him? "Well done my good and faithful servant." Pray to Him, cast your heart before Him and let Him search it. Let Him break you. Let Him show you things you haven't seen or maybe resisted! Call out to Him to let Him have all of your heart where nothing left is hidden. He calls us to this daily. Praise God that his grace covers us!

MB

What are the lessons God has for me in this passage of scripture?

_____

_____

_____

_____

How judgmental am I?

_____

_____

_____

_____

NOTES

_____

_____

_____

_____

_____

_____

_____

Prayer

_____

_____

_____

_____

Provisions By Faith

2 Corinthians 5:7 ‒ **"For we live by faith, not by sight."**

What do I see? When my son-in-law was talking with me about marrying my daughter, he said to me that one thing he knew he would never argue with her about was money. I laughed inside because to me it seemed inevitable. My wife and I have had struggles throughout our marriage over managing our expenses. The worry about our future creeps up on me sometimes and seems to take hold of more and more of my thoughts.

Matthew 6:31-34

So do not worry, saying, 'What shall we eat?' or 'What shall we drink?' or 'What shall we wear?' For the pagans run after all these things, and your heavenly Father knows that you need them. But seek first His kingdom and His righteousness, and all these things will be given to you as well. Therefore do not worry about tomorrow, for tomorrow will worry about itself. Each day has enough trouble of its own.

But faith tells me something very different......By faith I know that God has taken care of me thus far, and my wife, and my family. By faith I believe in His word. I read it and **believe** in it because He is the same always. He is constant, He is faithful to his promises, He is living, He watches over me (us), and He is a loving God, a loving father. He takes such good care of the birds of the air and flowers of the field and I know I am much more important to Him than they are. He has provided for me, actually in excess thus far. When I begin to worry, I set my mind on Him, the miracles He has done in our life (financial and otherwise), His promises, and His faithfulness. I know that He will provide for me as He has done so far. Lord, Abba Father, Thank you for your faithfulness.

I join you in prayer as you cast your burdens before Him. Bring to mind how He has brought you safely so far. Thank Him and praise Him for his faithfulness and for His abundant gifts. He is worthy to be praised for who He is.

MB

What are the lessons God has for me in this passage of scripture?

_____

_____

_____

_____

Where does my worry lie?

_____

_____

_____

_____

NOTES

_____

_____

_____

_____

_____

_____

_____

Prayer

_____

_____

_____

_____

Victory By Faith

2 Corinthians 5:7 - **"For we live by faith, not by sight."**

What do I see? There sure have been a lot of earthquakes lately, and I have heard it is likely we are going to have the 'big one' in our area soon. There are wars everywhere, famines, starving children, leaders that openly hate Americans. Our government doesn't seem to be able to get things done. The economy is a mess, not just in the US but in the world. There doesn't seem to be any answers to the problems. And there is another thing, why do all the children these days have so many allergies, and why is cancer so prevalent in young children? It just isn't right! The world is a mess!

John 16:33

I have told you these things, so that in me you may have peace. In this world you will have trouble. But take heart! I have overcome the world.

But faith tells me something very different........I know who I am in Christ and that we are greater than he who is reigning terror on earth. Can you imagine? By faith and belief in God's word I can overcome the evil one. And if that is true (and it is), how much more can the church do collectively? It can seem sometimes like we are losing the battle. But that is not the case because we know how it is all going to end. The battle, however is getting more intense, the lines more clear. But I know this: We win! We are to be victorious, and in fact we are considered to already be conquerors – no – we are actually "MORE THAN" conquerors. We need to be confident in our actions and at peace at the same time. Peace because He gives me peace and I know the end. But conquerors can't sit still, they are constantly moving forward. And I (we) must also.

As I stride along side of you in the fight, can we join in the following prayer? Lord, I need your help to see beyond circumstances and to know that I am truly more than a conqueror. Build my faith. Remind me to pray for the world around me and not just what is in **my** little world. Make your promises real to me. I want to know you and invite you to work in me. Lord, pour out your faith, hope, and love on me so that I can have more to give to others. Amen!

MB

What are the lessons God has for me in this passage of scripture?

_____

_____

_____

_____

What can I do to help overcome problems of this world/earth?

_____

_____

_____

_____

NOTES

_____

_____

_____

_____

_____

_____

_____

Prayer

_____

_____

_____

_____

Life By Faith

2 Corinthians 5:7 - "For we live by faith, not by sight."

What do I see? What is going on? I can't jump like I used to. I have more aches and pains. I get sick more frequently. I can't even run 2 miles without having to walk. I used to depend on sports for fun and more so, my feeling of accomplishment, success and even my self-worth. As a result it is how I spent all my free time. This old body just isn't what it used to be. But really - I am not that old... am I?

Psalm 73:26

My flesh and my heart may fail, but God is the strength of my heart and my portion forever.

But faith tells me something very different.....I know that the Lord in me can do way more than this failing frame can do. He can do exceedingly abundantly MORE THAN I can hope for or imagine, and He does. My desires never fulfilled me, just filled the day. Really, what good was winning (or losing more than I care to admit)? I am now running in the race of faith which has eternal value. He has a specific plan for me. When I lean on Him a new excitement fills me. I can be a part of His army and do things I never thought I had the courage to do. When I move in obedience there is a new joy and hope that fills me. I still can't run 2 miles (Who knows, maybe someday I will have an Elijah experience and run as fast as a horse, for His purpose). Oh Lord, let me obey you even more so. Use all of me. Use me up so I have nothing left. Amen.

MB

What are the lessons God has for me in this passage of scripture?

_____

_____

_____

_____

What can I do to stay focused on Gods strength in me?

_____

_____

_____

_____

NOTES

_____

_____

_____

_____

_____

_____

Prayer

_____

_____

_____

Grace

2 Corinthians 12:9-10

But He said to me, "My grace is sufficient for you, for my power is made perfect in weakness." Therefore I will boast all the more gladly about my weaknesses, so that Christ's power may rest on me. That is why, for Christ's sake, I delight in weaknesses, in insults, in hardships, in persecutions, in difficulties. For when I am weak, then I am strong.

Have you ever had a hardship or faced any difficulties?
Have you ever felt weak and discouraged?

Knowing just a little about the author helps to hear and understand some of his writings on these verses. Paul suffered hardship, but because he understood God's grace and purpose for his life, he kept pressing forward and he continues to impact the world even today. Are we able to grasp this truth and receive God's word?
"My grace is sufficient for you, for my power is made perfect in weakness."

Have you witnessed God's grace? I have. Soon after graduating, I found myself searching for a job and realizing that many others with much more experience and degrees were competing for that same job. Not only did I have minimal experience, but also minimal references to support my learned skills. At this point, I admitted my weakness and stood before God and believed wholeheartedly in His grace. Soon after, I boldly and in faith applied for that job, God opened the doors for me and gave me the job. I knew then that without a shadow of doubt that God had intervened on my behalf. This event most definitely reaffirmed me of not only His amazing grace, but of His unfailing love.

It is in weakness that we will mostly find God's grace. When we are able to admit that we can't do it on our own then God's grace is revealed to us and we are able to live productively. This verse teaches us to acknowledge our weakness in order to become strong. If we can just acknowledge our weakness, we then are able to live and enhance God's kingdom, we do this by reaching out to others and by extending His grace.
Would you admit today that God's grace is sufficient for you?
God provides His gracious serenity, courage and wisdom just when we need them most. Ask the Lord to provide you with His peace, boldness and insight necessary to carry out all of God's plans for you today.

RG

What are the lessons God has for me in this passage of scripture?

_____

_____

_____

_____

What are my weaknesses?

_____

_____

_____

_____

NOTES

_____

_____

_____

_____

_____

_____

Prayer

_____

_____

_____

_____

Man Card

Luke 11:5-9

Then Jesus said to them, "Suppose you have a friend, and you go to him at midnight and say, 'Friend, lend me three loaves of bread; a friend of mine on a journey has come to me, and I have no food to offer him.' And suppose the one inside answers, 'Don't bother me. The door is already locked, and my children and I are in bed. I can't get up and give you anything.' I tell you, even though he will not get up and give you the bread because of friendship, yet because of your shameless audacity he will surely get up and give you as much as you need.

Hebrews 4:16

Let us therefore come boldly to the throne of grace, that we may obtain mercy and find grace to help in time of need.

Ever confused that being a Christian man means you have to check your Man Card at the door? Too often humble and loving gets confused with timidity and weakness? Are we to become passive losing those characteristic of a man that God created us to be? Do we only play defense and never play offense? Absolutely not! We are to be bold in approaching God, asking him for good things with shameless audacity and forcefully advance his kingdom in the world we live! No weakness here! Mighty men of God carry a sword! Is your sword sharp?

Lord give me strength to seek you with shameless audacity. Give me strength to stand strong like the warrior you have called me to be. I am more than a conqueror! You open the doors of your throne to me so I can come boldly to receive your power and authority to be victorious. Lord, sharpen my mind so that I can contain the perfect word of God and share it appropriately with judgment and grace and authority. Amen!

LN

What are the lessons God has for me in this passage of scripture?

_____
_____
_____
_____

Is my sword sharp?

_____
_____
_____
_____

NOTES

_____
_____
_____
_____
_____
_____
_____

Prayer

_____
_____
_____
_____

Weary Wart

Galatians 6:9 NIV/KJ

Let us not become weary in doing good, for at the proper time we will reap a harvest if we do not give up/And let us not be weary in well doing: for in due season we shall reap, if we faint not

A powerful statement indeed! Our biggest reward is not on this earth.

Here is my problem....I am weak!! I am often weary (tired, fed up, done...) of doing good! Wanting to faint! It isn't the good I do for others outside my family. I don't think I have mighty expectations from others. Then why you ask? It's within the walls of my own home, I feel disrespected at times, like nobody cares about what I do, like my wife (who is pretty good about reminding me of what I don't do) couldn't care less about what I do.
Really!!
Well, maybe, if I do look at it from her point of view I could do more to be helpful, take the kids to do something so she could have some personal time! Or, I could show her more love! I could be available for more conversation time!

Don't give up! Don't faint! Be a servant! We are the men of our homes. Lead! Do it with compassion! Don't hear more than your wife is saying, don't put words into her mouth! We will reap a harvest!

KW

What are the lessons God has for me in this passage of scripture?

_____

_____

_____

_____

What makes me worry? What can I change in life to help it go away?

_____

_____

_____

_____

NOTES

_____

_____

_____

_____

_____

_____

_____

Prayer

_____

_____

_____

_____

Live in the Light

Psalm 27:1

1 The LORD is my light and my salvation— whom shall I fear? The LORD is the stronghold of my life— of whom shall I be afraid?

David had experiences that troubled him, just like you and I. He found himself in dark moments of his life, but in the midst of all that, he said "The Lord is my light and my salvation." When we are in the most difficult times (darkness) and somehow we receive light, it makes all the difference in the world. If you have been there, you would know that it is an awesome feeling. It is a joyful moment. It is obvious to me that David had an experience with God in order to make this statement. Not only did he say "the Lord is my light," but "my salvation and my stronghold."

Like David, I personally had an experience when I was troubled with that darkness. Having just graduated from college and with the responsibility of a wife and a new born, I found myself with no finances to move to a place where we needed to live and to find a job in my field of study. Yes, it seemed dark when I had no one near to ask for help and I had limited hope, but I was then reminded of this precise Psalm. I then got on my knees and said "the Lord is my light and my salvation." Soon after, we started packing and while paging through a college book of past years, God handed me a 100 dollar bill. Fell right out in my lap! Wow! That opened my eyes and ears and I heard His voice saying "Just trust in me, I will take you to where you need to be." I tell you today, God is so faithful!

Would you believe God revealed himself to David in times when he had no hope, in times of desperation, in times of fear and insecurity? God desires to do exactly that for you today. Would you courageously make this statement in faith today and trust Him with all that you have? Repeat this verse and believe in Him with all your heart.

RG

What are the lessons God has for me in this passage of scripture?

_____

_____

_____

_____

Am I hearing God clearly? Or at all?

_____

_____

_____

_____

NOTES

_____

_____

_____

_____

_____

_____

_____

Prayer

_____

_____

_____

_____

Get out of the Boat!

Matthew 14:24-33

About three o'clock in the morning Jesus came toward them, walking on the water. When the disciples saw him walking on the water, they were terrified. In their fear, they cried out, "It's a ghost!"
But Jesus spoke to them at once. "Don't be afraid," he said. "Take courage. I am here!"
Then Peter called to him, "Lord, if it's really you, tell me to come to you, walking on the water."
"Yes, come," Jesus said. So Peter went over the side of the boat and walked on the water toward Jesus. But when he saw the strong wind and the waves, he was terrified and began to sink. "Save me, Lord!" he shouted.
Jesus immediately reached out and grabbed him. "You have so little faith," Jesus said. "Why did you doubt me?"

Why look down and become afraid after you have already been walking on the water? Where is your faith? Peter's drop in faith seems all too familiar.
There is a gap in me that leaves me unfulfilled. It steals my peace and leaves me longing for more. Like a traveler that misses his home, I go through my days successful enough in checking the boxes of things needed to get done but I never accomplish satisfying the yearning that is at my core.
Filling this hole is essential to ever realizing peace and it is my own fault I have this condition. I know how it can be filled although for some unexplained reason I keep the cure at arms distance. The answer to my condition, the cure to my illness, is right in front of me and ready to be received by me. Yet, I stand in contradiction. I cling to my own illness, my own sickness, so tight while longing to face my cure.
I don't know much but I do know this: in me, there will always be brokenness. In Him there is healing, peace and wholeness. So what's the problem?
I fear what total surrender will require and what will transpire if I fully participate in receiving His direction over my life like that of a conductor over an orchestra. It would require complete removal of my opinion, submission of my pride and fears, a true dependence on Him through faith. Do I have enough faith and strength to take such a step without reverting back to a place of comfort that is unpeaceful but very familiar? Or, will His arms of grace really be enough to hold and support me in that place that is so peaceful and yet seemingly uncomfortable?
How thankful I am to know it is not about ME, or about my abilities, strength or capacity of faith. It is not about my bank account, my failures in the past or my current relationships. It is truly about taking a kernel of faith he has given me and in full submission and reliance, in faith, to say and mean, OK, Lord.

LN

What are the lessons God has for me in this passage of scripture?

_____

_____

_____

_____

How might I be keeping Jesus' grace just out of reach?

_____

_____

_____

_____

NOTES

_____

_____

_____

_____

_____

_____

Prayer

_____

_____

_____

_____

Be a Light

John 1:3-4

Through him all things were made: without him nothing was made that has been made. In him was life, and that life was the light of men. The light shines in the darkness, but the darkness has not understood.

The darkness will never understand, it will just make excuses to stay the way it is. Nothing can change it, help it, make it better, happier, less bitter, less angry, less prideful, less arrogant... the darkness wants to be hateful! The darkness loves miserable! The darkness wanted to be in charge, to be the boss! The darkness wanted to make everything! The darkness can't stand the light. Don't let it consume you!
The light though... the light is spectacular. The light is life. The light will set you free. The light has given you your very being, the air you breathe, your wife, your children, your happiness, your love... your everything! The light is your God! Live in the light. Be the light of God!

Every day everywhere I go I want to be a light! I don't go out and try to impress people with my biblical expertise, just live in contentment and joy. But when it really shows is in conflict. When you keep your head in a difficult situation is when people really notice a difference in you.

Be the light in the name of God! Love what you have been given'! Live in faith! Live in the light of the word of God!

KW

What are the lessons God has for me in this passage of scripture?

_____

_____

_____

_____

How do I respond in conflict?

_____

_____

_____

_____

NOTES

_____

_____

_____

_____

_____

_____

Prayer

_____

_____

_____

_____

More Than...

Romans 8:35-37

Who shall separate us from the love of Christ? Shall trouble or hardship or persecution or famine or nakedness or danger or sword? As it is written: "For your sake we face death all day long: we are considered as sheep to be slaughtered," NO, in all these things we are more than conquerors through him who loved us!!!

You have to read this a few times to grasp a true understanding of what is being said: We CAN face the challenges that the world will throw at us trying to separate us. That is what we face all day long. We are in a fight each day to stay in faith.
BUT NO!!
(Conquer- To overcome, dominate, overpower, defeat!!!)
We are more than conquerors with Christ!! C'mon! feel that this week!
MORE THAN CONQUERORS!
Often I'm feeling beat up, overwhelmed, the pressure of the constant needs on my time, feeling like I can't get any of my to do list done. I just pray! Lord strengthen me, help me to feel like you say I am more than a conqueror through your love!
Share that with your wife! Lead your household like a warrior. Be a servant to your family. I have had a long day, or I'm tired, or I can't miss this game! Those all start with I! Nothing can separate us from the love of our savior. Read this all week! Live this!

We are more than conquerors With God!
KW

What are the lessons God has for me in this passage of scripture?

_____

_____

_____

_____

What are my biggest challenges?

_____

_____

_____

_____

NOTES

_____

_____

_____

_____

_____

_____

_____

Prayer

_____

_____

_____

_____

How Will You be Remembered

Genesis 12:2, 3

"I will make you into a great nation and I will bless you; I will make your name great, and you will be a blessing. I will bless those who bless you, and whoever curses you I will curse; and all people on earth will be blessed through you."

God was speaking to Abraham! Not the United States or someplace in the Middle East. But to a single person, Abraham! Why? **Abraham dedicated his life to the Lord.** For that God promised him a legacy beyond his imagination.

More and more every day I am humbled. I am so overwhelmed with the fact that my eight year old daughter will grow up with a relationship with Christ her entire life! Something I only learned as a grown man of 35 years. It really makes me emotional. My 2 year old son as well. And then their children, and their children... Thank you Lord!

When is the last time we thought of the legacy we would leave? For our children, their children, their children...It's time to live by faith for we are saved by faith alone. Faith of a mustard seed even. So believe, see what God has in store for you and your family, dedicate your life to God first, He will make your name great, He will bless you, He will curse those who curse you, and all people on earth will be blessed through you. There is so much worth living for in this book, the Bible that is. Take it, read it, meditate on it. Let the Holy Spirit into your heart.

KW

What are the lessons God has for me in this passage of scripture?

_____

_____

_____

_____

What can my legacy be? What do I want my legacy to be?

_____

_____

_____

_____

NOTES

_____

_____

_____

_____

_____

_____

_____

Prayer

_____

_____

_____

_____

Patiently Wait

Psalm 40: 1-3

"I waited patiently for the LORD; He turned to me and heard my cry. He lifted me out of the slimy pit, out of the mud and mire; He set my feet on a rock and gave me a firm place to stand. He put a new song in my mouth, a hymn of praise to our God. Many will see and fear and put their trust in the LORD."

This Psalm reminds us who God is and what he so dearly wants for us. He wants to be totally 'entangled' in our lives and heart so that we will sing a renewed song of praise. Sometimes we need to wait patiently for Him, but more often I think He waits patiently for us. He wants the best for his children, to lift us out from the sinking sand (worries, concerns, and traps) that we have fallen into. He will carry our burdens and will set us free. I know this, because he has done that for me and continues to do so.

I have lived a life of another person. I lost myself in 1970 in 3rd grade when a teacher told me that I was stupid, lazy and unteachable. I wasn't stupid, I had a learning disability (dyslexia). But to an 8 year old little boy, I was stupid and I needed to hide it, and I did, throughout my whole life....until 2001 when I received Christ.

Through my life, I wore many masks No one was going to find out the real me. Through the years my masks got thicker and more confusing so that I eventually lost who I was. In the 1980's, during my teenage years of sex, drugs and rock & roll, I was living it and losing myself more and more. When I bottomed out in 2001 at 41 years of age, in the hospital, my pancreas poisoned from years of over consumption of alcohol, with the reality that I was an alcoholic, I knew that something needed to change. I had been using alcohol to mask who I thought I was, and it finally caught up to me. Jesus finally got my attention! My desperate response was, "HELP ME LORD, I am ready and willing and need You because **I can't do it by myself!**" I knew that if I didn't change my behavior, I would lose my soon to be wife, my job, and my life.
Jesus found me, crying out for help. Psalm 40: 1-3 is what Jesus has done for my life. Through the past 10 years I have taken all the masks off, one by one. I am joyfully pursuing my adventure with God. As the lyrics in the beautiful song Amazing Grace say " how sweet the sound...my chains are gone and I've been set free"... this sums up my life today. I am living day by day, for HIS purpose and for HIS glory. With Jesus' help, I have discovered who I am. And I can say that I truly like myself (yayah!) and have a confidence and a strong FAITH developed at Eastridge Church and through bible study. A faith that has brought me here to Hawaii, ready and able to do HIS work.
I am one HAPPY man.
Is there a place in your life where God is patiently waiting for you to let him in? A hurt, a failure, a relationship maybe, a habit? He is standing at the door and knocking. Won't you let him in? Won't you accept the incredible freedom and journey he has for you? Trust in him, it will be good! Pray!
MH

What are the lessons God has for me in this passage of scripture?

_____

_____

_____

_____

Is God waiting for me? Can I let him in?

_____

_____

_____

_____

NOTES

_____

_____

_____

_____

_____

_____

_____

Prayer

_____

_____

_____

_____

Listen

Proverbs 10:19

When words are many, sin is not absent, but he who holds his tongue is wise.

I don't care where you get this advice, it is good food. Fact is though, it is the word of God. Direct from the book of life, important to recognize just that. This is not a word from Confucius, to be taken or not. It is an important word of God to help us with living in His light and removing ourselves from our worldly thought process. 99% of the best "advise" you hear originated from the same place.

How often are we thinking of our response or comeback to what someone is saying while they're saying it? I actually laugh when I am doing that these days. I cannot count the number of times I have been saved by reflecting on this verse! Saved from saying something stupid and just making sure I hear the whole sentence before I respond in whatever the situation. It's not always a crisis or a bad conversation, just any conversation!

This week... listen! Then... speak life. The Holy Spirit is in us; Jesus used him and left us that counselor right in our hearts. Access that before your conversations. Pray that you will listen as opposed to offer your own wise words, that your pride will not stop you from hearing the truth. It will be noticeable throughout your day.

KW

What are the lessons God has for me in this passage of scripture?

_____

_____

_____

_____

When can I use this word from God?

_____

_____

_____

_____

NOTES

_____

_____

_____

_____

_____

_____

_____

Prayer

_____

_____

_____

_____

Give Your Best Effort

Joshua 1:8

Do not let this book of the law depart from your mouth; Meditate on it day and night, so that you may be careful to do everything written in it, then you will be prosperous and successful!

This might have been my first favorite! I thought: all I have to do is do what it says in the Bible and prosperity and success are mine?! We sometimes like to look at our favorite uplifting part of a scripture, in this verse it says "we will be prosperous and successful". Sometimes though we disengage from the how. In this passage we are called to meditate on the Bible day and night!

Besides that my ideas of prosperity and success have changed over the years, living a sinless life is quite impossible. I don't do anything radical: I'm not a drunk, no adultery, no murder... but maybe a little white lie here and there, or some disappointment, or irritation, get disgusted, bitter! Is that any way to respond to the things God has given me? Lord forgive me. I have to believe what it says and that my family is worth my best effort! So I continue to stay in the message and cast my pride (my biggest sin) at the feet of Jesus and live with high expectations in the word of God!!

Dedicate some time to the word of God. Starting with this verse this week.
Give your family your best effort!

KW

What are the lessons God has for me in this passage of scripture?

_____

_____

_____

_____

What can I change to make more time for Gods word?

_____

_____

_____

_____

NOTES

_____

_____

_____

_____

_____

_____

_____

Prayer

_____

_____

_____

_____

From The Ashes

Hosea 6:1-3 KJV

Come, and let us return unto the LORD: for he hath torn, and he will heal us; he hath smitten, and he will bind us up.
After two days will he revive us: in the third day he will raise us up, and we shall live in his sight.
Then shall we know, if we follow on to know the LORD: his going forth is prepared as the morning; and he shall come unto us as the rain, as the latter and former rain unto the earth.

This is old testament, if we turn from God he will let us go. He will teach us the error of our ways. A lot like being grounded if you broke the rules. Imagine how you might feel as a parent when your child disobeys. And I'm talking about just utter disobedience not just, no I don't want to take out the garbage. I'm talking about stole the car disobedience! He is a loving God through and through and always wants the best for us. We have to make the choice to come back though. It's called free will. But... If we are going to live in sin outside of the blessing of the Lord, well....we best be prepared! When were ready to repent He will be there to lift us from the pit and love you with compassion no earthly father has!
This is a special scripture for me as I've felt torn and tattered in the past few years. My business was losing money, and my marriage and health were suffering. I turned to the Lord for strength, and He has answered: my finances have been supernaturally healed, my health is wonderful, and my marriage is now a source of joy, not pain.
Try it yourself. Turn to the Lord. He wants us to count on Him in our time of need whatever that may be.

BA

What are the lessons God has for me in this passage of scripture?

_____

_____

_____

_____

When can I leave in Gods hands?

_____

_____

_____

_____

NOTES

_____

_____

_____

_____

_____

_____

_____

Prayer

_____

_____

_____

_____

Judge Not

Romans 2:1-8

You, therefore, have no excuse, you who pass judgment on someone else, for at whatever point you judge another, you are condemning yourself, because you who pass judgment do the same things. Now we know that God's judgment against those who do such things is based on truth. So when you, a mere human being, pass judgment on them and yet do the same things, do you think you will escape God's judgment? Or do you show contempt for the riches of his kindness, forbearance and patience, not realizing that God's kindness is intended to lead you to repentance? But because of your stubbornness and your unrepentant heart, you are storing up wrath against yourself for the day of God's wrath, when his righteous judgment will be revealed. God "will repay each person according to what they have done." To those who by persistence in doing good seek glory, honor and immortality, he will give eternal life. But for those who are self-seeking and who reject the truth and follow evil, there will be wrath and anger.

Those people are on a dark spiral downward. But if you think that leaves you on the high ground where you can point your finger at others, think again. Every time you criticize someone, you condemn yourself. It takes one to know one. Judgmental criticism of others is a well-known way of escaping detection in your own sins. But God isn't so easily diverted. He sees right through all such smoke screens and holds you to what you've done. You didn't think did you, that just by pointing your finger at others you would distract God from seeing all your misdoings??

Look inside yourself to see what you need to work on and don't criticize someone else as it will condemn you. It was just yesterday when I was notified that I was doing this. Obviously God wanted to make sure I was listening as well as I should, so He figured He would reiterate the point to me during our 1:1 time. And I listened! Heavenly Father, help me to speak encouragement and truth and not criticism. Help me to be the man, the husband, the father, the employee that you need me to be. I repent and ask you for forgiveness.

PD

What are the lessons God has for me in this passage of scripture?

_____

_____

_____

_____

Three simple steps to help refrain from being judgmental of others.

_____

_____

_____

_____

NOTES

_____

_____

_____

_____

_____

_____

_____

Prayer

_____

_____

_____

_____

We Are All Equals

John 13:12-15

When he had finished washing their feet, he put on his clothes and returned to his place. "Do you understand what I have done for you?" he asked them. "You call me 'Teacher' and 'Lord,' and rightly so, for that is what I am. Now that I, your Lord and Teacher, have washed your feet, you also should wash one another's feet. I have set you an example that you should do as I have done for you."

If Jesus doesn't separate himself from his disciples, whom after what they had witnessed over the last couple years should be laying their lives down before him. How can we separate ourselves from our peers? By job title, by financial status, or any other status. And don't forget he washed Judas Iscariots feet also (the deceiver)!! Knowing full well what he had intentions of doing!!

When I started my own flooring company I ended up with employees of course. From training to this day they are introduced as my partner to the home/business owner when we arrive on a job together.

Throw down your pride. Treat everyone as your equal!! Being judgmental is a sin. Don't do it! You don't know how the guy collecting change on the freeway exit ended up there. Be polite to the car wash attendant. Be polite to your waiter.

KW

What are the lessons God has for me in this passage of scripture?

_____

_____

_____

_____

How did I do last week in my judgment of others?

_____

_____

_____

_____

NOTES

_____

_____

_____

_____

_____

_____

_____

Prayer

_____

_____

_____

_____

Forget About It

Proverbs 19:11

A man's wisdom gives him patience; it is to His glory to overlook an offense.

More wise proverbs, My favorite part of this short scripture is "it is to His glory", who's? Gods! To do what? Exercise some patience! Really not that tough unless your pride won't let you.

I put these thoughts to paper (well computer) on September 8th 2010. I don't do " full vent anger" but I can do irritation, disgust, disappointment, aggravation etc... pretty well. And pretty well kept under control today. Filled with patience, compassion, and even prayer for those who look to offend. And even those who offend without even knowing. Example- in conversations with a friend of mine he knew that my wife and I struggled with our relationship at times. We have had some giant hurdles to overcome, things I pray most people will never have to deal with. One day he stood me up on a volunteer activity, I sent him a sarcastic text (my usual) he sent back a rude text, referencing my relationship issues with my wife. At first I was offended! Then, I thought, he doesn't know the facts, just some comments made in simple conversation, hence, he wouldn't have any idea how offensive those comments could have been. So... how can I take offense.

And you of course know people speak without thinking? Don't be offended! It isn't worth the thought.

KW

What are the lessons God has for me in this passage of scripture?

_____

_____

_____

_____

Who has offended me? How do I overlook such offenses?

_____

_____

_____

_____

NOTES

_____

_____

_____

_____

_____

_____

Prayer

_____

_____

_____

Speak, From an Undivided Heart

Psalms 86:11

Teach me your way, O Lord, and I will walk in your truth; give me an undivided heart, that I may fear your name.

One of my biggest struggles in life is the "white lie." You know, the lie that isn't meant to hurt anyone but you tell it to protect or lessen the pain of the truth. Or just say something doesn't bother you when it really does. Too many times I find myself not delivering the truth, delivering a portion of the truth, or I change the truth, in other words, I lie. This causes problems because delivering part of the truth or not delivering it at all leaves the truth in my heart causing a divided heart.

If we rely on the Lord's teachings because of His undivided heart, how can we accept the fullness of the Spirit in ourselves if our own hearts are divided? I use the "white lie" because I fear that the respondent will not receive the message with an open heart. I want to be loved, appreciated, and admired by my wife. I want these things so much that I've developed a fear of confrontation. I fear confrontation which leads to poor communication, altogether avoiding conversation to avoid confrontation. I basically shut down after holding truth in my heart for too long. If I continue to fear confrontation more than I fear the "Wrath of God" than I am being disobedient and I am not honoring the Lord. Telling a "white lie" to please the flesh does not honor God. If I am not honoring God I'm living in sin which gives the devil access to my heart and mind which then creates a divided heart and evil thoughts. I can deliver the truth but the conviction that comes with truth should be delivered by the Holy Spirit. If I keep the truth in my heart and let it divide my heart the devil will attack the truth and when the time is right the devil will show me the way to deliver conviction with fire on my tongue. This creates a situation where it is flesh vs. flesh and not Spirit vs. spirit. Letting the truth sit in my heart to please the flesh ultimately spoils it. Once it spoils it cannot be delivered without blame or conviction because that truth is no longer blessed by the Spirit, it is controlled by evil.

I hope that understanding this will allow me to live life to the fullest. When I want to say something but I don't, I'm shutting out the Spirit and stunting my own growth. If I am going to be what God has planned for me I cannot do it if there is anything but truth in my life. I have learned something very valuable and I know in my heart that the truth will set me free.

God bless all of you and hopefully my lesson learned can be knowledge that you can use in your life.

RS

What are the lessons God has for me in this passage of scripture?

_____

_____

_____

_____

What can I do to speak truth gently instead of holding onto it?

_____

_____

_____

_____

NOTES

_____

_____

_____

_____

_____

_____

_____

Prayer

_____

_____

_____

_____

Arrrgh!

Philippians 2:14-16

Do everything without grumbling or arguing, so that you may become blameless and pure, "children of god without fault in a warped and crooked generation." Then you will shine among them like stars in the sky as you hold firmly to the word of life....

What!! No more irritation, annoyance, frustration, discontentment, disrespect? Throw down the pride?
I would have to live in all that happiness, joyfulness, contentment?
Try this week not to add words to what your wife is saying. Try not to be irritated with the kids!
How about our daily commute to work? You know at the roundabout, dropping the kids at school. Or... in line at the grocery store, or trying to find someone to show you were something is at the Home Depot (or your favorite place of annoyance).
It is amazing what happens when you put in a little effort! And why? "To become blameless and pure, children of God in a warped and crooked generation." Then we will be the light!
In the Message Bible it says "do everything readily and cheerfully-no bickering allowed! Go out into the world uncorrupted, a breath of fresh air in this squalid and polluted society! Provide people with a glimpse of good living and of the living God..." WOW!!
I have to add this testimony. As I was randomly choosing and practicing reading each of these verses for a week prior to the release of the book this week popped up. My first thought.... NO, I want to argue and grumble, I don't want to be joyful this week. You see, the prior week had been long and tough. I wasn't ready to give it up, I wanted sympathy for all that I had to do and deal with. What a perfect time to read this life application verse and realize that I could overcome this warped and crooked society and live in the love of God!
This is a great message from a great book!! Read this everyday this week!
God Bless you and your family.

KW

What are the lessons God has for me in this passage of scripture?

_____

_____

_____

_____

How do I really let the Holy Spirit out and fight the negativity?

_____

_____

_____

_____

NOTES

_____

_____

_____

_____

_____

_____

Prayer

_____

_____

_____

_____

Peace Comes with Prayer

Philippians 4:4-7 KJV

Rejoice in the Lord always: and again I say, Rejoice.
Let your moderation be known unto all men. The Lord is at hand.
Be careful for nothing; but in everything by prayer and supplication with thanksgiving let your requests be made known unto God.
And the peace of God, which passeth all understanding, shall keep your hearts and minds through Christ Jesus.

In other translations "be careful for nothing" translates as " be anxious about nothing"
In some translations, the word moderation is translated as gentleness.
I need to work on that. To me, there is great significance in verses 6 and 7 "And the peace of God, which passeth all understanding, shall keep your hearts and minds through Christ Jesus." Unlike other places in the Gospel, it doesn't promise that we will get what we pray for, it's just telling me to let my needs be known, but that the reward will be peace of mind, not necessarily the specific outcome I desire but at least piece of mind.

This past year has been a real test of my faith. My wife had some serious communication problems, we've even spent a great deal of time apart_. I often spoke without a gentle spirit, at least. Last year I began praying for the infilling of the Holy Spirit. I also had my Christian brothers praying for me, One event in particular was a Christian Businessman's Lunch. After those mighty men of God prayed for me, I received a wonderful peace of mind, that has been my constant companion since then. At times, it's even a physical sense of warmth in my chest. It's very difficult for me to get angry now. Frustrations pass quickly and don't overwhelm my emotions. As momentary anger passes, it's replaced by calm peace of mind, even a little amusement at my petty reaction. Satan is having a hard time ruling my thoughts and emotions. Christ has been victorious. I'm reading the word now with two chapters of Old Testament, two of New Testament, and one chapter of Philippians each day. I've also found that reading aloud has really allowed God's word to fill my mind and heart.

Read and believe with me this week. Call on the Lord of all creation He is waiting for you! Leave all things to Him who loves us. Pray for Gods peace and understanding.

BA

What are the lessons God has for me in this passage of scripture?

_____

_____

_____

_____

What does the word rejoice mean to me?

_____

_____

_____

_____

NOTES

_____

_____

_____

_____

_____

_____

_____

Prayer

_____

_____

_____

_____

No, thank you?

Matthew 26:39-44
Going a little farther, he fell with his face to the ground and prayed, "My Father, if it is possible, may this cup be taken from me. Yet not as I will, but as you will."
Then he returned to his disciples and found them sleeping. "Couldn't you men keep watch with me for one hour?" he asked Peter. "Watch and pray so that you will not fall into temptation. The spirit is willing, but the flesh is weak."
He went away a second time and prayed, "My Father, if it is not possible for this cup to be taken away unless I drink it, may your will be done."
When he came back, he again found them sleeping, because their eyes were heavy. So he left them and went away once more and prayed the third time, saying the same thing.

I find comfort in Jesus' distress at God's will while praying in the garden and I appreciate so much more that he really was a man as seen in this instance. I also find comfort in his begging or pleading in prayer to God, "if it is possible, may this cup be taken from me." While ultimately Jesus followed God's will, was obedient and became sacrifice for your sins and mine, I appreciate that he pressed God on something he really didn't want to do. We see throughout scripture Jesus fulfilling God's will in seamless harmony. This is a nice glimpse of Jesus praying to God, "Are you sure? Can I skip this one? No? Ok."

My own example of such an issue, every time someone tells me of a worry, or a pain, or concern in their life I get the urge to pray for them right then and there. That is definitely God's prompting. It's not life or death but it has been one of those things I've had to grow into to be obedient. To stop and pray no matter where or what is sometimes not the most comfortable feeling. We are called to pray for one another throughout the Bible.

Have you ever found yourself in a situation you didn't like and asked God to remove you or change the situation? Has God ever led you to do something you really didn't want to do? Did you feel guilty because you didn't do it? While we must be obedient in our heart and in our actions, I'm encouraged that we can go before God and reason with him. And even if God doesn't change his mind, he may just increase our faith and dependence upon him enough to get us through the situation.

LN

What are the lessons God has for me in this passage of scripture?

_____

_____

_____

_____

Am I praying for Gods will?

_____

_____

_____

_____

NOTES

_____

_____

_____

_____

_____

_____

_____

Prayer

_____

_____

_____

_____

No Fear

Isaiah 41:10
So do not fear, for I am with you; do not be dismayed, for I am your God. I will strengthen you and help you; I will uphold you with my righteous right hand.

Frequently we find ourselves feeling some sort of fear. Just to mention a few, as a child, the fear of being left behind, as young adults, the fear of not belonging and potentially today, the fear of uncertainty. Why do we fall into the enemy's favorite weapon? Could it be because we fail to listen to God's word?

When I meditate on this verse and I ponder on how it has impacted my life. The words even today, are like the sweet aroma of a spring morning, like a refreshing sound of a running river that cleanses all my fears away. The God of the universe, the risen Christ speaks to me and also confirms to me that he is with me, that he will strengthen and help me, and that he will uphold me with his righteous right hand.

Have you ever heard more encouraging words? When we objectively listen to these words, we can boldly face the future knowing that God is with us every step of the way. Would you ponder that this week? God tells you "fear not, I am with you." When you and I choose to receive this message, nothing can hold us back from living a fruitful life.

RG

What are the lessons God has for me in this passage of scripture?

_____

_____

_____

_____

Where can I use the strength of God right now? What are my fears?

_____

_____

_____

_____

NOTES

_____

_____

_____

_____

_____

_____

_____

Prayer

_____

_____

_____

_____

Gods Way First

2 Timothy 1:7

For the Spirit God gave us does not make us timid, but gives us power, love and self-discipline.

Just as one of my fellow writers mentioned in a previous week, I to want so much to be loved, appreciated and even admired by my wife. But I can't make it the goal of my life! I cannot in any way sacrifice what God wants me to do so that I can do what I think will please my wife so that I will receive what I need or want from her. This is being disobedient to God. My hope must be in God alone, not in my wife. Because...
by faith I know He can complete our marriage and me. Looking inward toward my desires I must depend on the power of the Holy Spirit and the cleansing Christ offers to overcome my own sin of pride, selfishness, and stubbornness. Am I so great that I should put my desires before God's? Is God so small that He can't fulfill my desires? I am the apple of His eye! Do I have faith in this knowledge or do I just say it? No more hopes empty of Christ, but by faith and with thanksgiving I receive God's power, love and self-discipline to complete God's mission for my marriage and my life as HE would have it!
Read this verse with me this week and put all your faith, hope, trust and belief in our Lord and Savior!! Be bold! Live in the word!
MB

What are the lessons God has for me in this passage of scripture?

_____

_____

_____

_____

What steps can I take to let God be my guiding light?

_____

_____

_____

_____

NOTES

_____

_____

_____

_____

_____

_____

_____

Prayer

_____

_____

_____

_____

We Lack Nothing

Psalms 34:4-9

I sought the Lord, and He answered me; He delivered me from all my fears. Those who look to Him are radiant; their faces are never covered with shame. This poor man called, and the Lord heard him; He saved him out of all his troubles. The angel of the Lord encamps around those who fear him, and He delivers them. Taste and see that the Lord is good; blessed is the one who takes refuge in Him. Fear the Lord, you His holy people, for those who fear him lack nothing.

All through the Bible God is calling us to take relationship with him. We are his children. He wants us to look to him for answers. But just like our parents he will let us on our own, we have free will. Psalms 34 shows clearly what God wants from us, Obedience! To fear the Lord is to LOVE the Lord. Again I hear PRAY! I sought the Lord, those who look to Him, this poor man called, blessed is the one who takes refuge in Him. How do we do this? By Prayer! What happens? He answered me, our faces are never covered with shame, He hears us and saves us from our troubles, He sends an angel to watch over us, WE LACK NOTHING!

Oh the difference in a day when I spend some morning time seeking the Lord! It is powerful.

I see the difference in my wife when I really spend that 5 minutes minimum in prayer over her alone. I'm not trying to say every prayer gets answered but that peace of mind is so comforting. Thank you Lord!

There is only 22 verses in Psalms 34, read them all as often as you can this week. Or...at least these six. And believe it, live in faith! Pray that God will get you that raise, resurrect your relationship with your wife, your children, your boss. If there are troubles let God in. His hand is extended, wanting to grab hold and help you up. From the edge of the cliff all the way down. He will even pull you from the miry clay no matter how long you have been there. Read this again and again!

KW

What are the lessons God has for me in this passage of scripture?

_____

_____

_____

_____

Where can I start?

_____

_____

_____

_____

NOTES

_____

_____

_____

_____

_____

_____

Prayer

_____

_____

_____

_____

Judging Others

Acts 3:19

Repent, then, and turn to God, so that your sins may be wiped out, that times of refreshing may come from the Lord,

Matthew 7:1-5

"Do not judge, or you too will be judged. For in the same way you judge others, you will be judged, and with the measure you use, it will be measured to you. Why do you look at the speck in your brother's eye and pay no attention to the plank in your own eye? How can you say to your brother, 'Let me take the speck out of your eye,' when all the time there is a plank in your own eye? You hypocrite, first remove the plank from your own eye."

In Acts, we see a few more such examples of needing to have a radical change in our lives, but we first need to repent and turn away from our sinful nature and acts. We also need to look inside ourselves and see what is needed to be done and what we need to work on. We see that it says in Matthew 7 "remove the plank from your own eye, and then you will see clearly to remove the speck from your brother's eye."

So Lord I turn to you and ask you Lord God, for wisdom, for discernment, and for strength that I may walk in your ways all the days of my life. And, Lord, I come this morning seeking your face. I don't want to stay out in the hallway, but I want to enter into the Most Holy place and be with you, thanks to the sacrifice of your son Jesus, I know that I am now able to come in and speak with you. I also know that as I look for opportunities and knock, that you will open the right doors to allow me to fulfill your will and plan in my life. I'm thanking You with all my heart. You pulled me from the brink of death, my feet from the cliff-edge of doom. Now I stroll at leisure with you in the sunlit fields of life. Lord I turn to you and I give you all the praise and all the glory in Jesus' Holy name. Amen.

PD

What are the lessons God has for me in this passage of scripture?

_____

_____

_____

_____

My faults and flaws.

_____

_____

_____

_____

NOTES

_____

_____

_____

_____

_____

_____

_____

Prayer

_____

_____

_____

_____

He Hears

Deuteronomy 32:1-4   KJV

Give ear, O ye heavens, and I will speak; and hear, O earth, the words of my mouth. My doctrine shall drop as the rain, my speech shall distil as the dew, as the small rain upon the tender herb, and as the showers upon the grass: Because I will publish the name of the LORD: ascribe ye greatness unto our God. He is the Rock, his work is perfect: for all his ways are judgment: a God of truth and without iniquity, just and right is He.

Give ear O ye heavens, hear, O earth, the words of my mouth. And what do I hear in this mighty and powerful message? Attribute success to the Lord's hand.

When I cried out to heaven for help, the Lord answered quietly. Slowly repairing all the sources of misery and stress in my life. My own efforts could not have achieved the healing in my business, body, or marriage. I'm surrounded by my loving Christian family and friends who have nurtured me through this time of trials. Even encounters with strangers have been a blessing. I met a homeless man in Victoria. I had been trying my hand at oil painting. He asked to have a look at my feeble effort. It turned out he was a graphic artist. He was able with a few suggestions to vastly improve my painting. He plays guitar for tips in the Harbor, and played some wonderful songs for me. As we talked, I learned he was a Christian, and without my asking, He prayed for an army of warrior Angels to surround and protect me.

I praise the Lord for a merciful God that hears my prayers, and answers with more than I could have asked for.

Give an ear to the Lord this week. Listen to what he is saying. It is always good, if it's bad it is not from God. It is that simple!

BA

What are the lessons God has for me in this passage of scripture?

_____

_____

_____

_____

What is God telling me that I need to hear?

_____

_____

_____

_____

NOTES

_____

_____

_____

_____

_____

_____

Prayer

_____

_____

_____

_____

Be Strong & Courageous

Joshua 1:5-9

"No one will be able to stand against you all the days of your life. As I was with Moses, so I will be with you; I will never leave you nor forsake you. Be strong and courageous, because you will lead these people to inherit the land I swore to their ancestors to give them. Be strong and very courageous. Be careful to obey all the law my servant Moses gave you; do not turn from it to the right or to the left, that you may be successful wherever you go. Keep this Book of the Law always on your lips; meditate on it day and night, so that you may be careful to do everything written in it. Then you will be prosperous and successful. Have I not commanded you be strong and courageous. Do not be afraid; do not be discouraged, for the Lord your God will be with you wherever you go."

God has a promised land for you. He has a plan that is greater than anything we could ever ask or imagine. It is a place filled with milk and honey, a place where there is enough to meet all your needs. So step out and receive it. Know that God goes before you and no man will be able to stand before you. Know that He will be with you every step of the way and He will never fail you or forsake you. Be strong, be confident, and be of good courage for God is calling you to lead others into their inheritance. God is so determined that He repeated and emphasized it saying "Be strong and very courageous" so that we will be obedient to God's law and will in our lives.

God has an incredible way of being there to speak the exact thing I need to hear. He knew exactly what I was going through and spoke to me through my morning time with Him as I read His Word. As bigger challenges came my way and taller mountains to climb appeared, His Word would speak hope and encouragement to me so that I would be encouraged heading out of my home and start into work. Listening to Christian music on the way into work fills my heart with joy and praise. And provides me with a heart and mind that is filled with hope. To keep my day started on a high God is the key and trusting and praying that He goes before me, to prepare in advance the work He has planned for me, allows me to walk into every situation knowing He is big enough to work it all out for His glory.

The best way to stay connected is to make sure you are in relationship with God, you are spending time with Him, you are talking with Him throughout the day, and you are reading His Word and consider what He is speaking to you through it. This will make your way prosperous and provide you wisdom and success. And one last time he re-emphasizes: "Have not I commanded you? Be strong and courageous. Do not be afraid, do not be discouraged, for the Lord your God will be with you wherever you go."

PD

What are the lessons God has for me in this passage of scripture?

_____

_____

_____

_____

Area's in my life I could use Gods courage and strength?

_____

_____

_____

_____

NOTES

_____

_____

_____

_____

_____

_____

_____

Prayer

_____

_____

_____

_____

Superman

Matthew 5:14-16

You are the light of the world. A city on a hill cannot be hidden. Neither do people light a lamp and put it under a bowl. Instead they put it on a stand, and it gives light to everyone in the house. In the same way let your light shine before men, that they may see your good deeds and praise your father in heaven

1st verse- YOU! Are the light of the world! The light of the WORLD!! This isn't just motivation from a friend; it is the word of God. That is what he thinks of you, and wants you to acknowledge this. Say it with me. I am the light of the world! Say it a few times. Makes me feel like... Superman!

I ask you, do you think Superman had his troubles? Kryptonite, maybe... Lex Luthor. But besides what he had as far as personal battles he still had to save the world! God isn't asking us to save the world, wouldn't mind our participation, but he wants us to be a light to shine before men, that they may see our good deeds! Not tell of our good deeds, but in our actions, our manner, our language. People will notice a difference.
What is this light? The Holy Spirit! I think if you get to know someone young or old(er) you will find they battle the same issues as you and I! How we handle them could be that light, that Holy Spirit guidance.

Can you shelve your pride, your anxiety, your disappointments this week? Don't fall into the trap of complaining about your wife, your kids, your job, heck the weather. Make the choice!
You are the light of the world!
KW

What are the lessons God has for me in this passage of scripture?

_____

_____

_____

_____

Who do I know that I can show this light to now?

_____

_____

_____

_____

NOTES

_____

_____

_____

_____

_____

_____

_____

Prayer

_____

_____

_____

_____

Reach Out

Proverbs 25:11-14   KJV

A word fitly spoken is like apples of gold in pictures of silver.
As an earring of gold, and an ornament of fine gold, so is a wise reprover upon an obedient ear.
As the cold of snow in the time of harvest, so is a faithful messenger to them that send him: for he refresheth the soul of his masters.
Whoso boasteth himself of a false gift is like clouds and wind without rain.

Proverbs are a great source of concentrated advice for living in the Light. This one reminds me how powerful are our words, for good or evil.
I'm taking time to be friendly to those I meet in my daily life. Grocery store clerks, bank tellers, whoever I encounter. One easy way is to ask about their name. That's easy if it's a common name, or I try to guess their birth place from their accent. No one has gotten mad if I'm off by a continent or two. I've met bank tellers from Siberia, Turkey, and Brooklyn. They love telling me about their hometowns, and I learn fascinating things. Did you know there are White Mountain Lions in Siberia?
A friendly word can brighten their day, and it sure brightens mine. One banker is now helping trace my family tree, something I've wanted to do for years. I believe our role is to be salt and light in a bland and dark world.
Try not to be so "busy" you can't find time to speak a good word unto someone.
BA

What are the lessons God has for me in this passage of scripture?

_____

_____

_____

_____

Where can I start speaking a good or kind word?

_____

_____

_____

_____

NOTES

_____

_____

_____

_____

_____

_____

Prayer

_____

_____

_____

_____

Cast Your Cares

Psalms 55:22

Cast your cares on the Lord and he will sustain you; he will never let the righteous fall.

Our God has a lot to say in this short verse.
PRAY! Give over your worries, your troubles, your doubts, cast them at the feet of our Lord and savior. He (God) will sustain you, guide you, watch over you, and leave his angels in charge over you. Thank you Lord!

Righteous is such an enormous thought, I could never consider myself such, but....I do live forgiving so that I may be forgiven, and I do live my life for God! I do know He is my life's blood and He will sustain me and never let me fall. This is great to remember as my family and I struggle to keep order in our home, spiritually, emotionally, financially....Every morning, Lord be with me this day, give me strength I can only find in you. I cannot do it on my own.

Will you read this verse with me each day this week? Cast your cares upon the Lord, pray for him to intercede in your life, in your home with your wife and children, at work with your boss and co-workers. Have faith, BELIEVE!!
KW

What are the lessons God has for me in this passage of scripture?

_____

_____

_____

_____

Where can I use Gods sustaining spirit the most?

_____

_____

_____

_____

NOTES

_____

_____

_____

_____

_____

_____

Prayer

_____

_____

_____

_____

Pass the Word

1 Peter 3:15

But in your hearts revere Christ as Lord. Always be prepared to give an answer to everyone who asks you to give the reason for the hope that you have. But do this with gentleness and respect,

This is my guide for giving testimony. For me, one of the keys, "to every man that asks you." To me this tells me that you can't force Christianity down someone's ears. They have to ask you. Then my role is to be prepared, by spending time in the Word. I've only begun in the last couple of years to have the courage to share my faith. I started with strangers as I was traveling, then worked up to my brother-in-law, and finally, the hardest, my father. I was blessed that my father accepted Christ at age 94, two weeks before the Lord took him Home. When I look at pictures of my Mom and Dad (She died in 1984), I'm warmed by the thoughts that they are together again. I'm blessed that my mother, and her parents were believers and always prayed for me and guided me back to the path.

                                 BA

What are the lessons God has for me in this passage of scripture?

_____
_____
_____
_____

What am I doing to save souls?

_____
_____
_____
_____

NOTES

_____
_____
_____
_____
_____
_____
_____

Prayer

_____
_____
_____
_____

A Final Thank You

Isaiah 46:4 NLT

"I will be your God throughout your lifetime—until your hair is white with age. I made you, and I will care for you. I will carry you along and save you."

A healthy definition of love is crucial to understanding the central message of the Bible. According to the Bible, love is not confined to sexuality, nor is it primarily a feeling at all. The Bible teaches that love is a commitment. Therefore, it is not dependent on good feelings, but on a consistent and courageous decision to extend oneself for the well-being of another. That commitment then produces good feelings, not the other way around.
Jesus became the perfect demonstration of God's unconditional love for us by laying down his life for our benefit.

God has truly been there throughout my lifetime. Even when I ignored his presence, not intentionally but still ignored him. He has given me a life I could not earn. Now to think he will continue to be there until my hair is white! WOW! He will care for me and carry me!! Why is it hard for me to grasp? Even as our children age we want them to stand on their own two feet. Truly God wants us to understand the love He has for us. No matter what!

Can you show your own family that kind of love? No matter what!

PD

What are the lessons God has for me in this passage of scripture?

_____

_____

_____

_____

Can I love unconditionally? To the end?

_____

_____

_____

_____

NOTES

_____

_____

_____

_____

_____

_____

_____

Prayer

_____

_____

_____

_____

Phil Davidson
42 years old
Married 14 yrs
3 Anointed children 2 girls/1 boy as God promised
Program Manager

Richard Shoemaker
35 yrs old
Married 12 yrs
3 children all girls, 13, 10, 8
Quality Assurance Supervisor

Robert Gomez
48 yrs old
Married 28 yrs
4 children 25yrs to 16 yr old girl
Software Engineer

Mark Borys
  Yrs old
Married   yrs
3 children, 4 grand children

Michael Hedwall
50 yrs old
Married 10 yrs
3 grown children
Moved recently to Hawaii to teach men the word of God

Bob Arnold
60 yrs old
Married 21 yrs
No children
Financial planner/Tax preparation specialist

Ken Wenner
47 yrs old
Married 15 yrs
4 children- 22yrs, 21yrs, 8 yrs, almost 3yrs
Founder/Director Be More With Jesus

Luke Neil
38 yrs old
Married 11 yrs
2 children 6 yr old son, 4 yr old daughter
Sales Representative

www.ingramcontent.com/pod-product-compliance
Lightning Source LLC
Chambersburg PA
CBHW031536040426
42445CB00010B/562